GUITAR
TAB
EDITION

Stereopho

CW00594798

WORD GETS AROUND

polygram music publishing limited

Exclusive Distributors:
Music Sales Limited
8/9 Frith Street,
London W1V 5TZ,
England.
Music Sales Pty Limited
120 Rothschild Avenue,
Rosebery, NSW 2018,
Australia.

Order No. AM952237
ISBN 0.7119.7101.3

This book © Copyright 1997
by PolyGram Music
Publishing Limited.

Visit the Internet Music Shop at
http://www.musicsales.co.uk

Music arranged by Kit Morgan.
Music processed by Digital Music Art.

Printed in the United Kingdom by
Caligraving Limited, Thetford, Norfolk.

Your Guarantee of Quality:
As publishers, we strive to produce
every book to the highest commercial standards.
The music has been freshly engraved and, whilst endeavouring to
retain the original running order of the recorded album,
the book has been carefully designed to minimise awkward page turns
and to make playing from it a real pleasure.
Particular care has been given to specifying acid-free, neutral-sized
paper made from pulps which have not been elemental chlorine bleached.
This pulp is from farmed sustainable forests
and was produced with special regard for the environment.
Throughout, the printing and binding have been planned to ensure a sturdy,
attractive publication which should give years of enjoyment.
If your copy fails to meet our high standards, please inform us
and we will gladly replace it.

Music Sales' complete catalogue describes

thousands of titles and is available in full colour sections by subject,

direct from Music Sales Limited.

Please state your areas of interest and send a cheque/postal order for

£1.50 for postage to: Music Sales Limited, Newmarket Road,

Bury St. Edmunds, Suffolk IP33 3YB.

guitar tablature explained

guitar music can be notated three different ways: on a musical stave, in tablature, and in rhythm slashes

RHYTHM SLASHES are written above the stave. Strum chords in the rhythm indicated. Round noteheads indicate single notes.

THE MUSICAL STAVE shows pitches and rhythms and is divided by lines into bars. Pitches are named after the first seven letters of the alphabet.

TABLATURE graphically represents the guitar fingerboard. Each horizontal line represents a string, and each number represents a fret.

4th string, 2nd fret   1st & 2nd strings   open D chord
                              open, played together

definitions for special guitar notation

SEMI-TONE BEND: Strike the note and bend up a semi-tone (1/2 step).

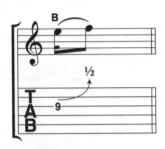

WHOLE-TONE BEND: Strike the note and bend up a whole-tone (whole step).

GRACE NOTE BEND: Strike the note and bend as indicated. Play the first note as quickly as possible.

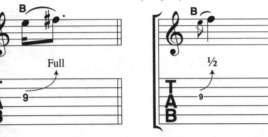

QUARTER-TONE BEND: Strike the note and bend up a 1/4 step.

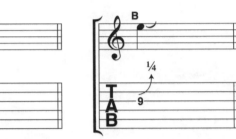

BEND & RELEASE: Strike the note and bend up as indicated, then release back to the original note.

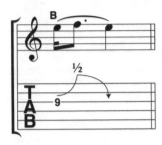

COMPOUND BEND & RELEASE: Strike the note and bend up and down in the rhythm indicated.

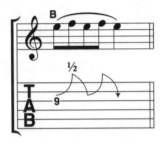

PRE-BEND: Bend the note as indicated, then strike it.

PRE-BEND & RELEASE: Bend the note as indicated. Strike it and release the note back to the original pitch.

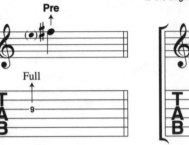

UNISON BEND: Strike the two notes simultaneously and bend the lower note up to the pitch of the higher.

BEND & RESTRIKE: Strike the note and bend as indicated then restrike the string where the symbol occurs.

BEND, HOLD AND RELEASE: Same as bend and release but hold the bend for the duration of the tie.

BEND AND TAP: Bend the note as indicated and tap the higher fret while still holding the bend.

VIBRATO: The string is vibrated by rapidly bending and releasing the note with the fretting hand.

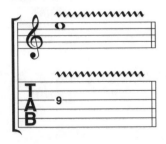

HAMMER-ON: Strike the first (lower) note with one finger, then sound the higher note (on the same string) with another finger by fretting it without picking.

PULL-OFF: Place both fingers on the notes to be sounded, Strike the first note and without picking, pull the finger off to sound the second (lower) note.

LEGATO SLIDE (GLISS): Strike the first note and then slide the same fret-hand finger up or down to the second note. The second note is not struck.

NOTE: The speed of any bend is indicated by the music notation and tempo.

4

SHIFT SLIDE (GLISS & RESTRIKE): Same as legato slide, except the second note is struck.

TRILL: Very rapidly alternate between the notes indicated by continuously hammering on and pulling off.

TAPPING: Hammer ("tap") the fret indicated with the pick-hand index or middle finger and pull off to the note fretted by the fret hand.

PICK SCRAPE: The edge of the pick is rubbed down (or up) the string, producing a scratchy sound.

MUFFLED STRINGS: A percussive sound is produced by laying the fret hand across the string(s) without depressing, and striking them with the pick hand.

NATURAL HARMONIC: Strike the note while the fret-hand lightly touches the string directly over the fret indicated.

PINCH HARMONIC: The note is fretted normally and a harmonic is produced by adding the edge of the thumb or the tip of the index finger of the pick hand to the normal pick attack.

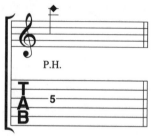

HARP HARMONIC: The note is fretted normally and a harmonic is produced by gently resting the pick hand's index finger directly above the indicated fret (in parentheses) while the pick hand's thumb or pick assists by plucking the appropriate string.

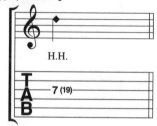

PALM MUTING: The note is partially muted by the pick hand lightly touching the string(s) just before the bridge.

RAKE: Drag the pick across the strings indicated with a single motion.

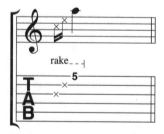

TREMOLO PICKING: The note is picked as rapidly and continuously as possible.

ARPEGGIATE: Play the notes of the chord indicated by quickly rolling them from bottom to top.

SWEEP PICKING: Rhythmic downstroke and/or upstroke motion across the strings.

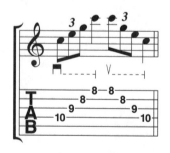

VIBRATO DIVE BAR AND RETURN: The pitch of the note or chord is dropped a specific number of steps (in rhythm) then returned to the original pitch.

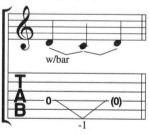

VIBRATO BAR SCOOP: Depress the bar just before striking the note, then quickly release the bar.

VIBRATO BAR DIP: Strike the note and then immediately drop a specific number of steps, then release back to the original pitch.

additional musical definitions

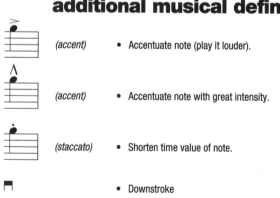

(accent) • Accentuate note (play it louder).

(accent) • Accentuate note with great intensity.

(staccato) • Shorten time value of note.

• Downstroke

• Upstroke

D.%. al Coda

D.C. al Fine

tacet

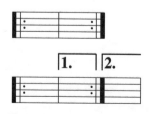

• Go back to the sign (%), then play until the bar marked *To Coda* ⊕ then skip to the section marked ⊕ *Coda*.

• Go back to the beginning of the song and play until the bar marked *Fine* (end).

• Instrument is silent (drops out).

• Repeat bars between signs.

• When a repeated section has different endings, play the first ending only the first time and the second ending only the second time.

NOTE: Tablature numbers in parentheses mean: 1. The note is sustained, but a new articulation (such as hammer on or slide) begins.
2. A note may be fretted but not necessarily played.

a thousand trees

words by kelly jones. music by kelly jones, richard jones & stuart cable.

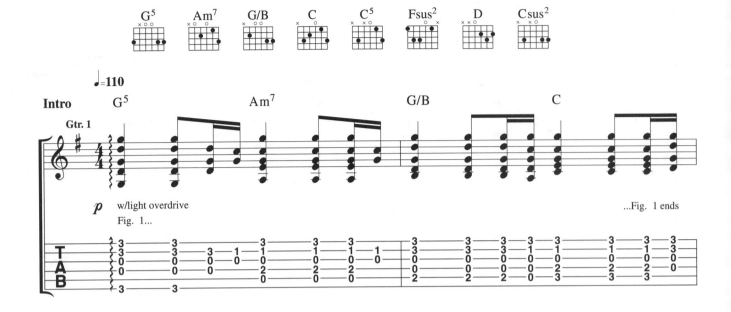

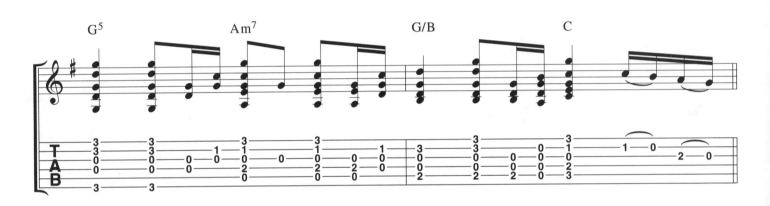

Scouts' hall, at the foot-ball, where the wise we trust are paid,— they all hon-our his name,—

— did a lot for the game,— he had his name knocked up a-bove the sports ground gates, now they're

rip-ping them down,— stam-ping the ground,— pic-ture ga-thers dust in the bar in the lounge, it takes—

— one tree— to make a thou-sand ma-tches, on-ly ta-kes— one match— to

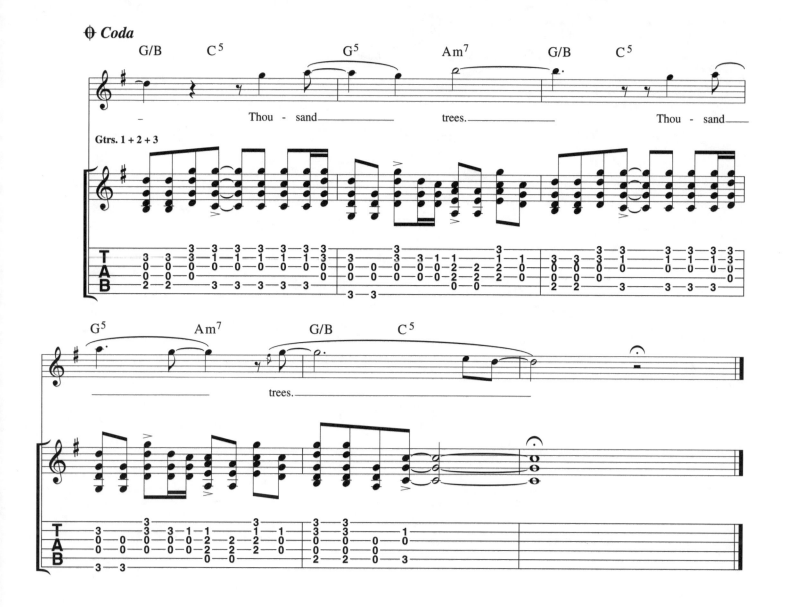

⊕ *Coda*

Thou - sand_____ trees._____ Thou - sand_____

_____ trees._____

Verse 4:

(In the) school yard
Change room
Playing fields
Bathroom
Phonebox
Office blocks
Corners turned around
They keep doubting the flame
Tossing the blame
Got his name knocked up above the
Sports ground gates
Now they're Ripping them down
Stamping the ground
Picture gathers dust in the
Bar in the lounge
It takes
(One tree to make a thousand matches)

looks like chaplin

words by kelly jones. music by kelly jones, richard jones & stuart cable.

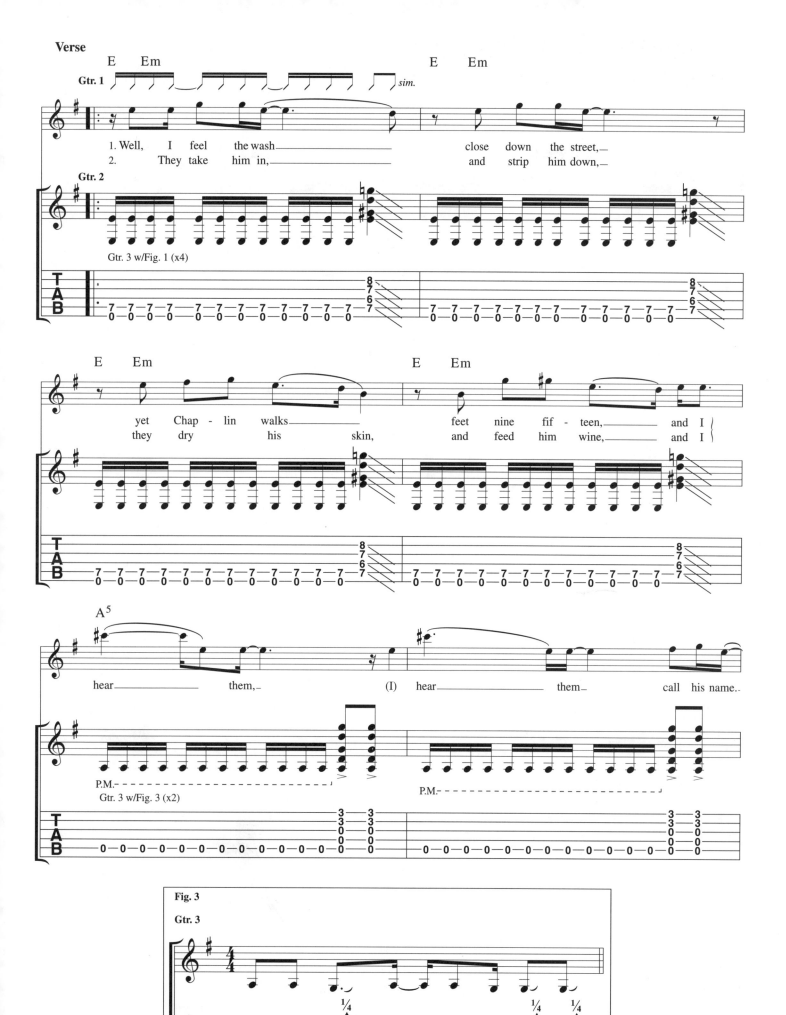

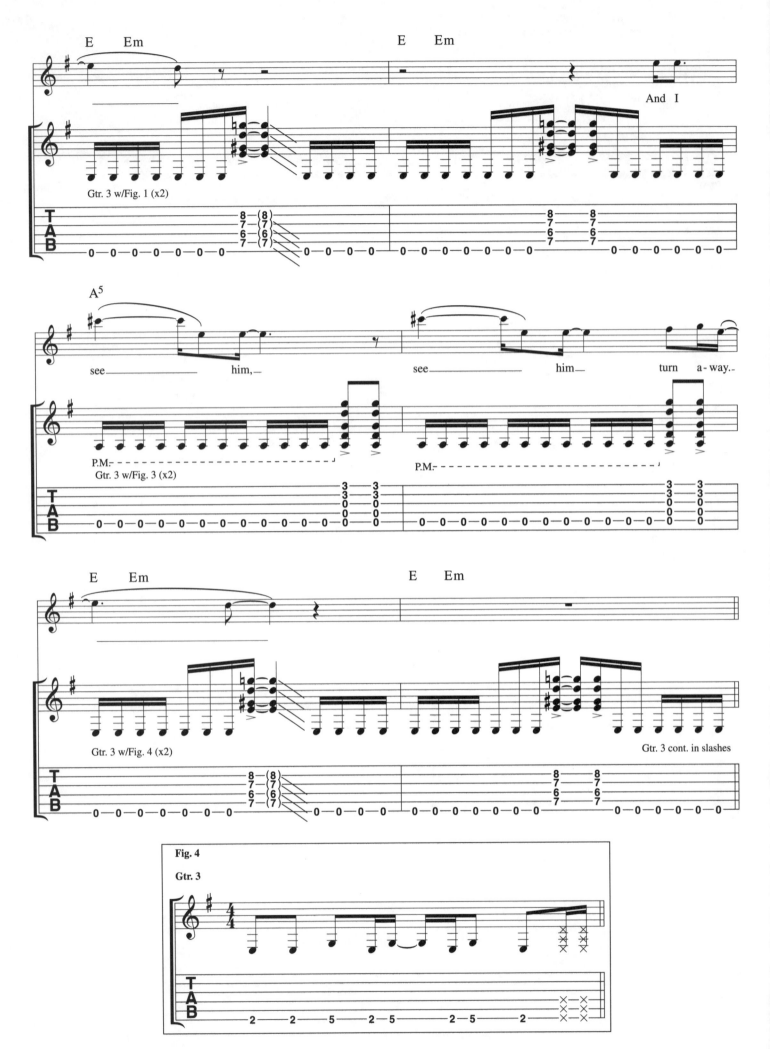

more life in a tramps vest

words by kelly jones. music by kelly jones, richard jones & stuart cable.

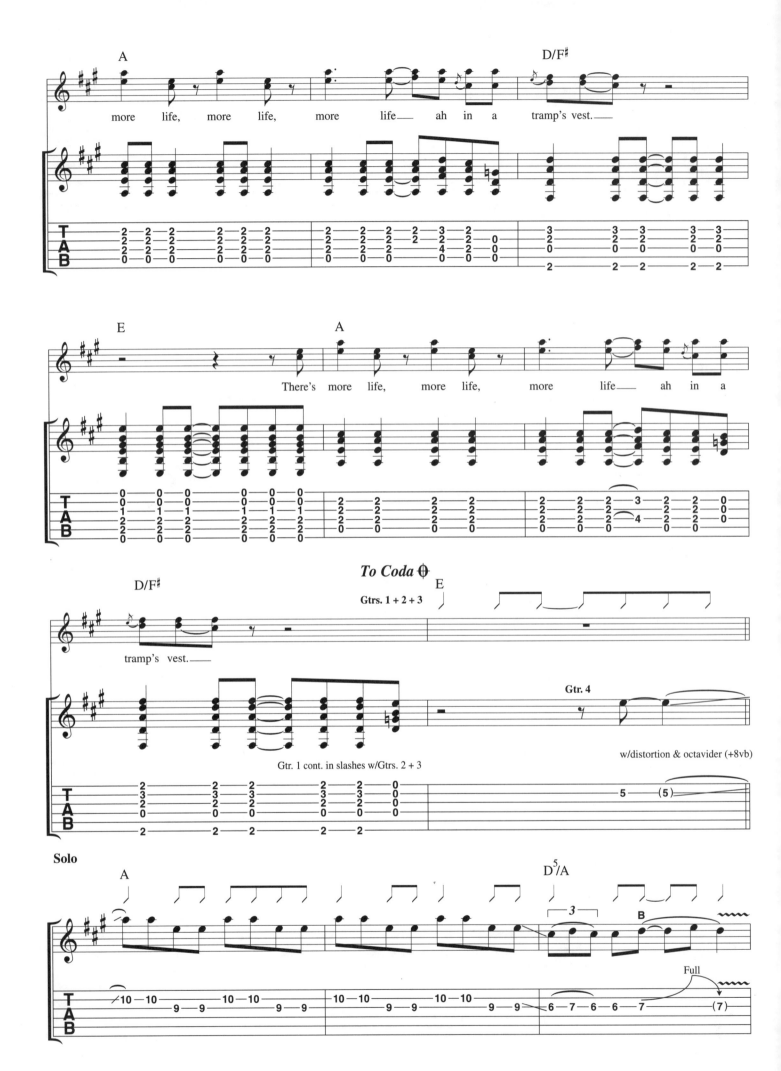

more life, more life, more life— ah in a tramp's vest.—

There's more life, more life, more life— ah in a

To Coda ⊕

Gtrs. 1 + 2 + 3

tramp's vest.—

Gtr. 1 cont. in slashes w/Gtrs. 2 + 3

Gtr. 4

w/distortion & octavider (+8vb)

Solo

Verse 3

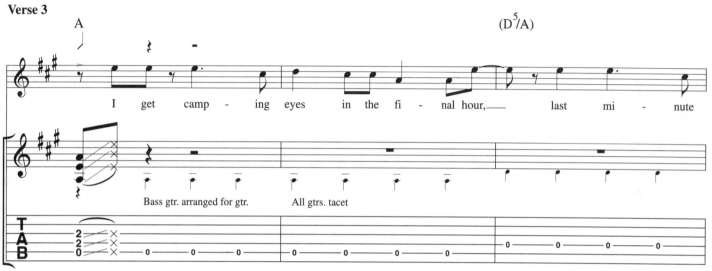

I get camp - ing eyes in the fi - nal hour,___ last mi - nute

Bass gtr. arranged for gtr.   All gtrs. tacet

D.%. al Coda
No repeat

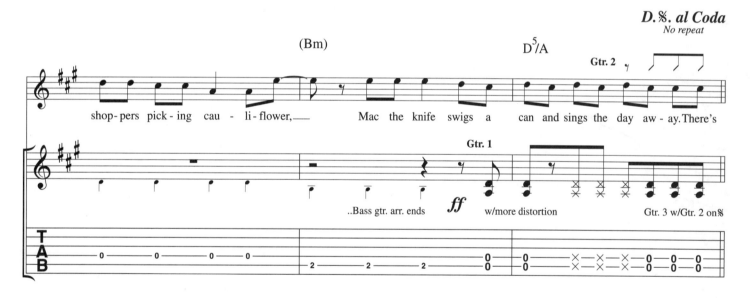

shop - pers pick - ing cau - li - flower,___ Mac the knife swigs a can and sings the day aw - ay. There's

Gtr. 1

..Bass gtr. arr. ends   *ff*   w/more distortion   Gtr. 3 w/Gtr. 2 on %

⊕ *Coda*

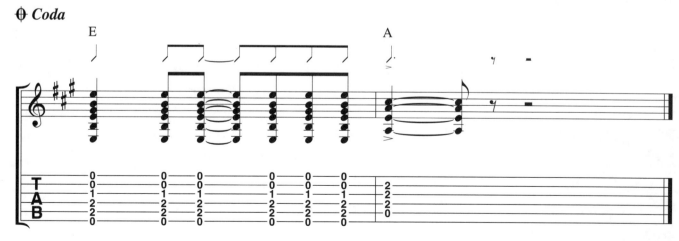

local boy in the photograph

words by kelly jones. music by kelly jones, richard jones & stuart cable.

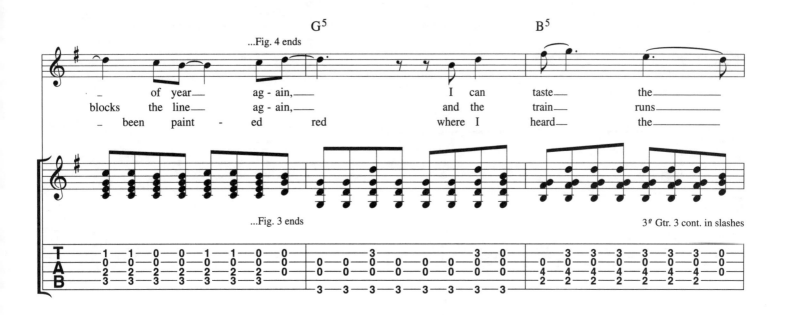

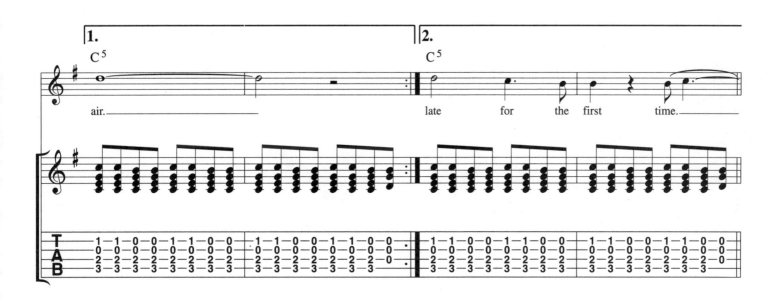

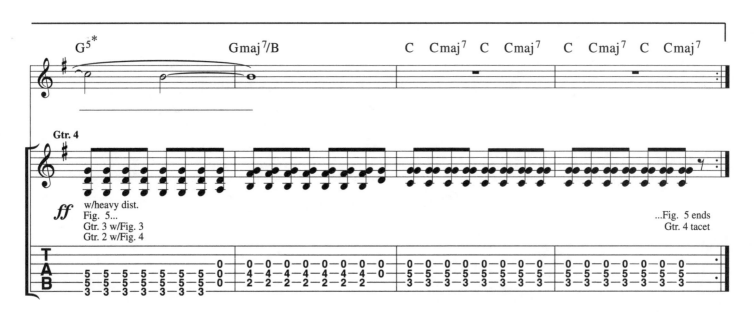

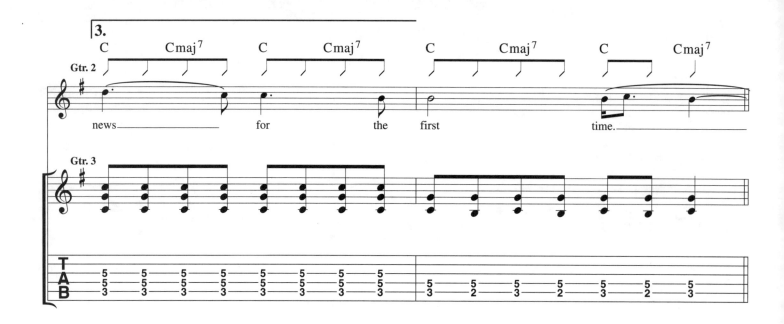

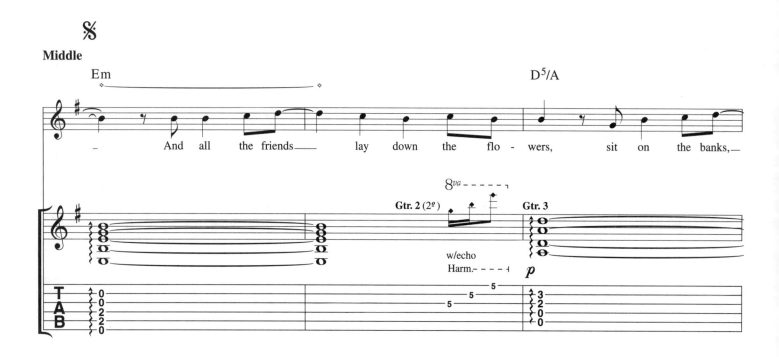

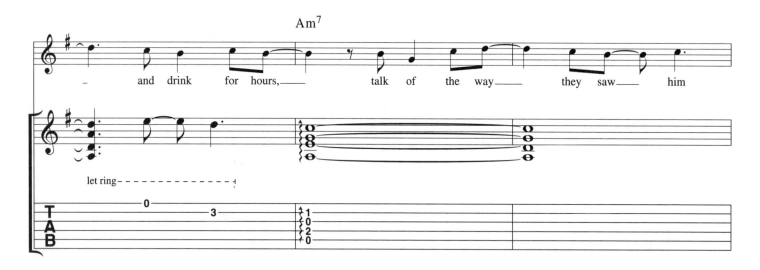

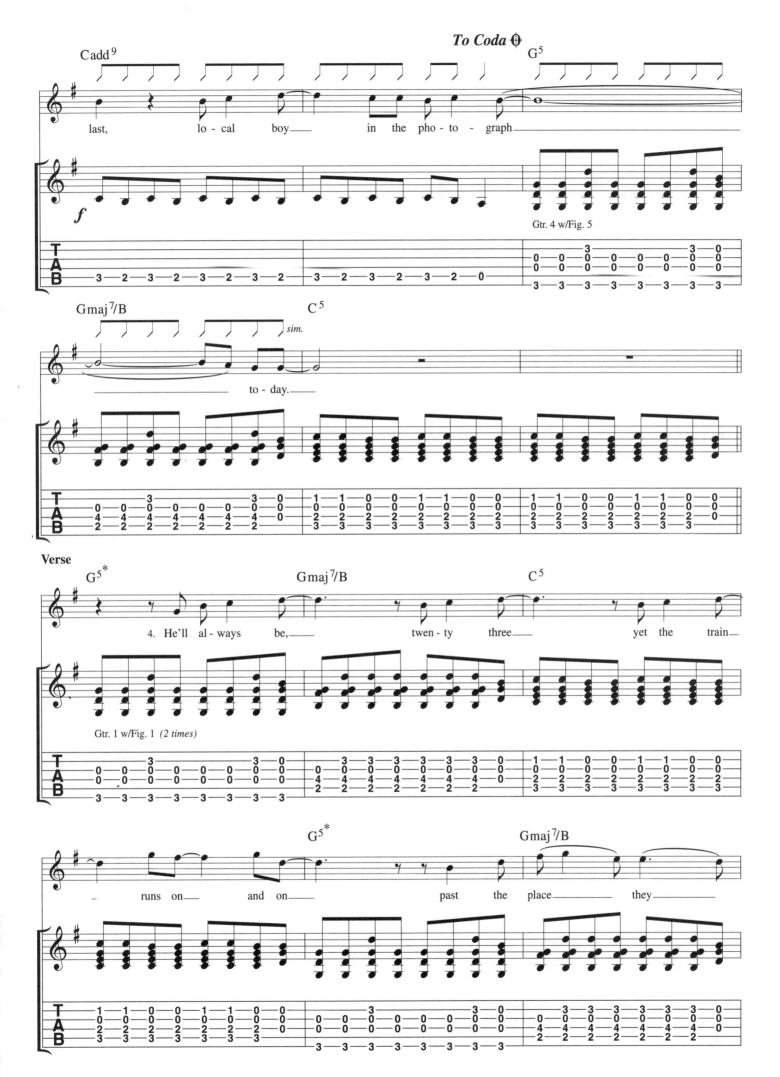

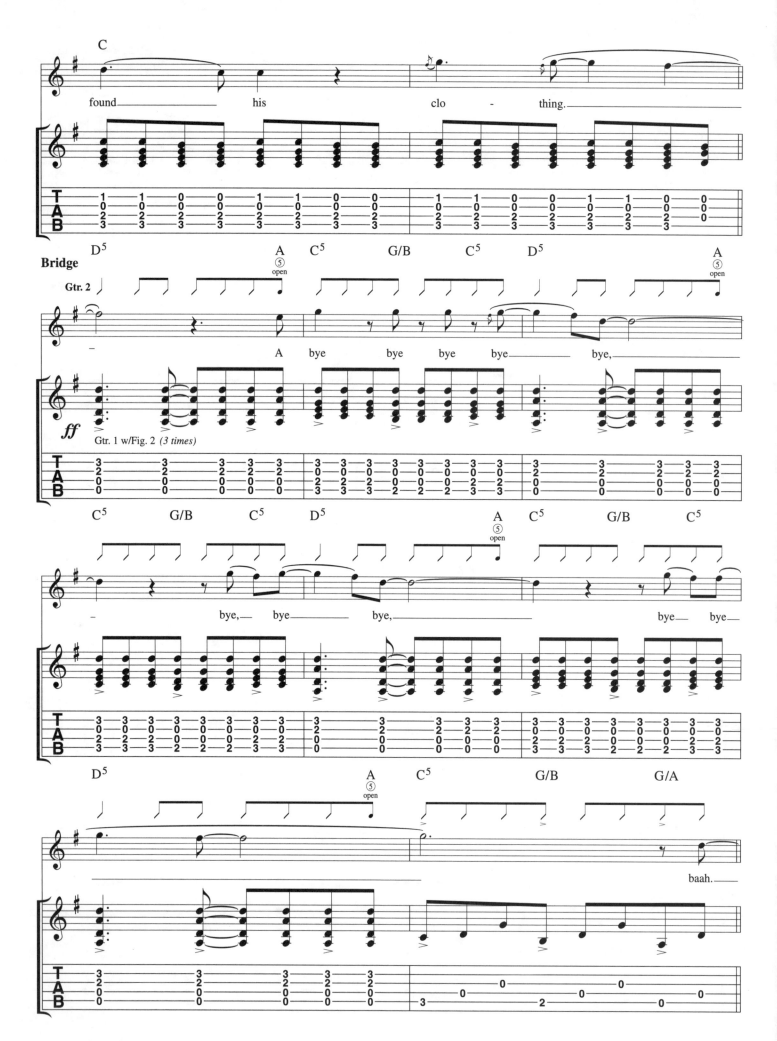

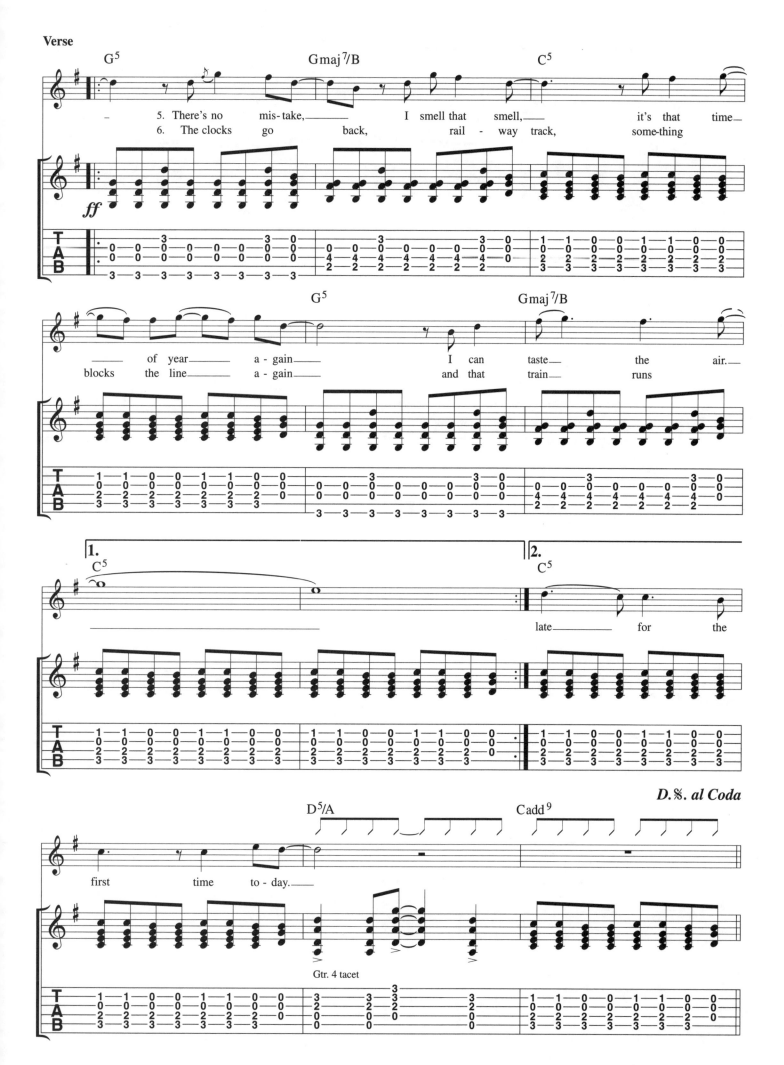

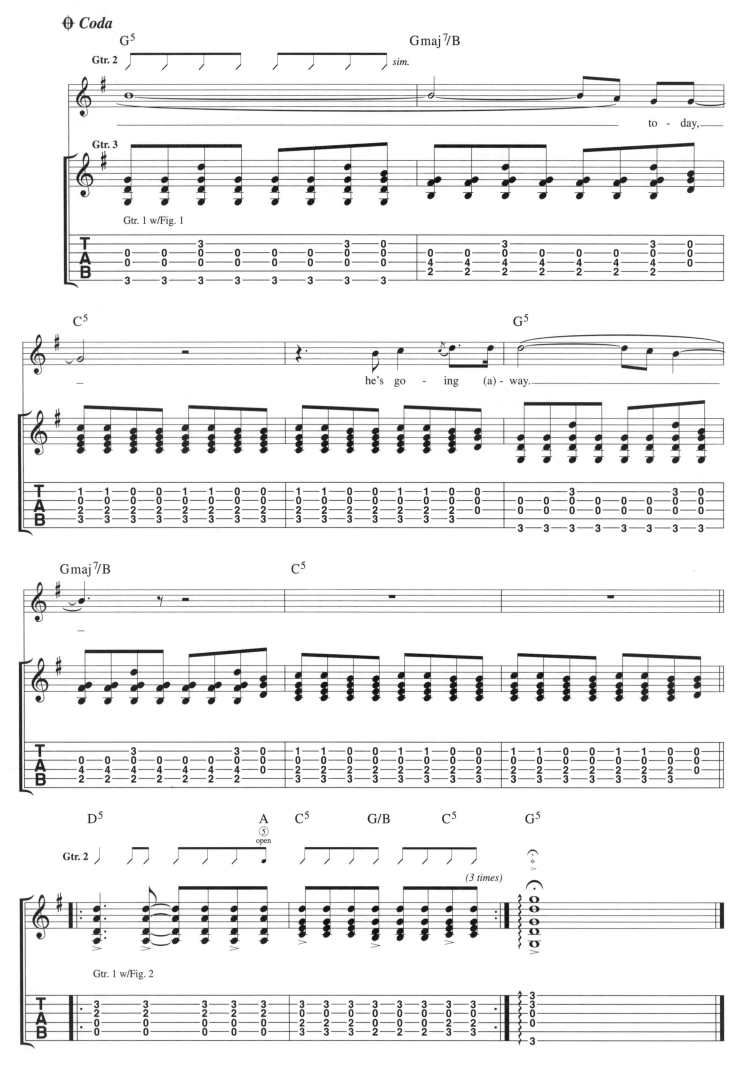

traffic

words by kelly jones. music by kelly jones, richard jones & stuart cable.

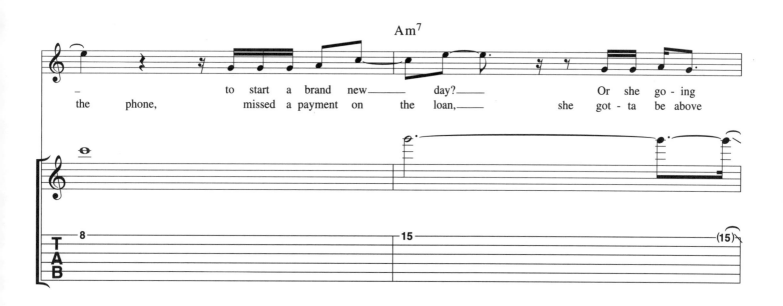

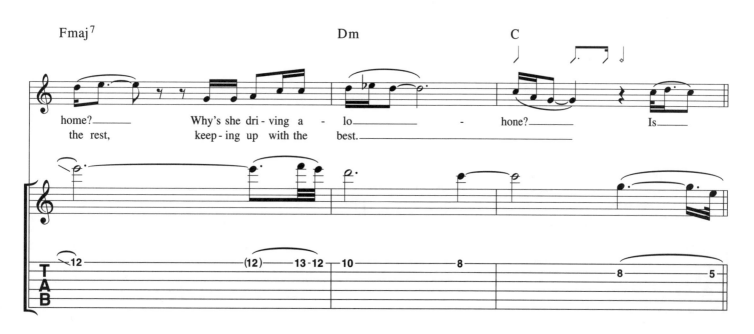

Chorus

Solo

Wait ta - bles for a crook who wrote a hard - back_____ book. __ D'you teach kids how to_____

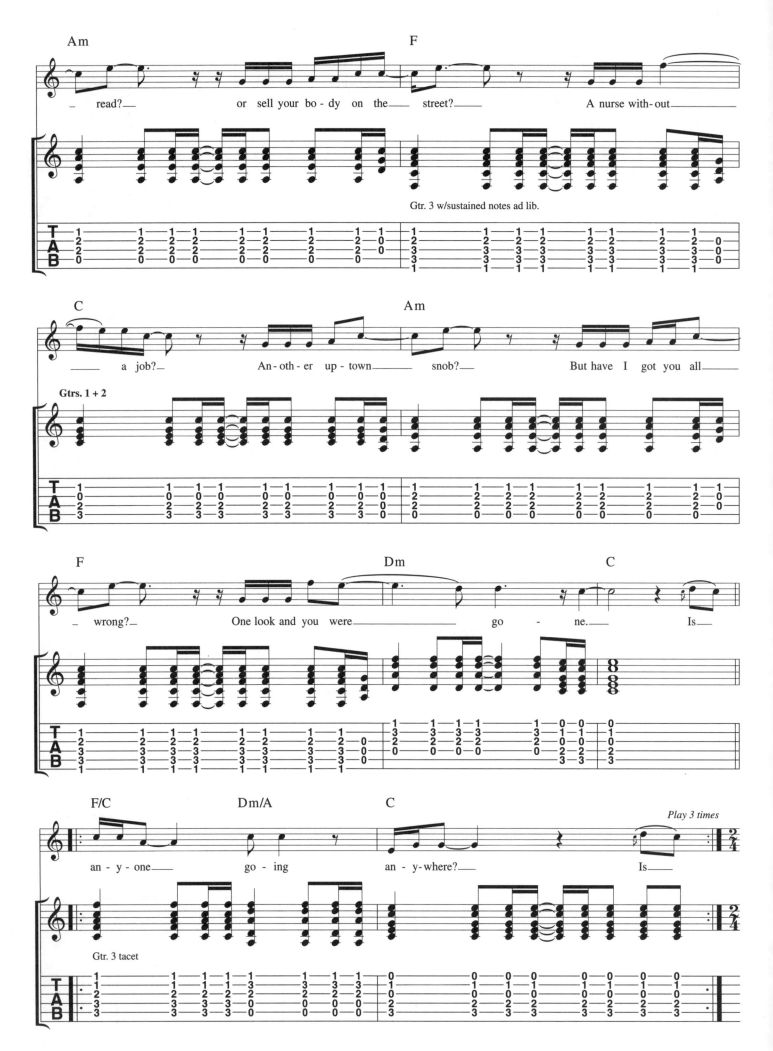

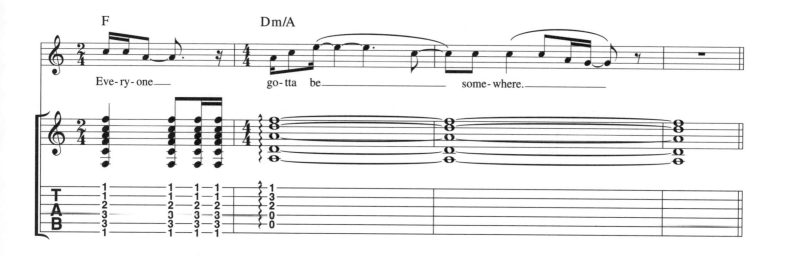

Eve-ry-one___ go-tta be___ some-where.___

Outro

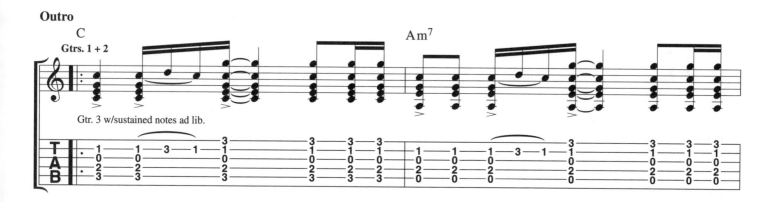

Gtr. 3 w/sustained notes ad lib.

1. 2. 3.

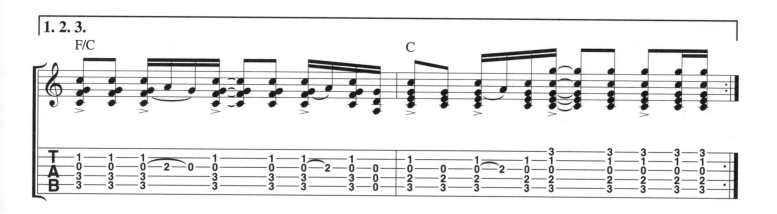

4.

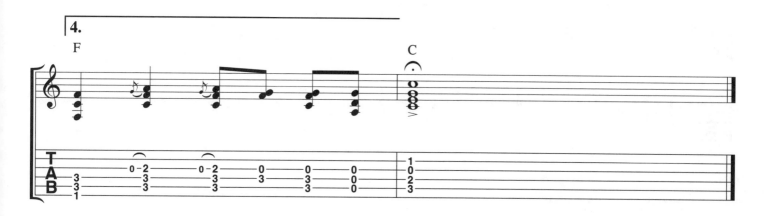

not up to you

words by kelly jones. music by kelly jones, richard jones & stuart cable.

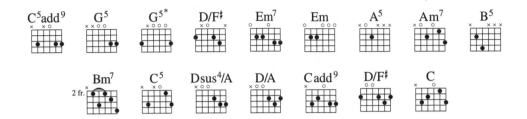

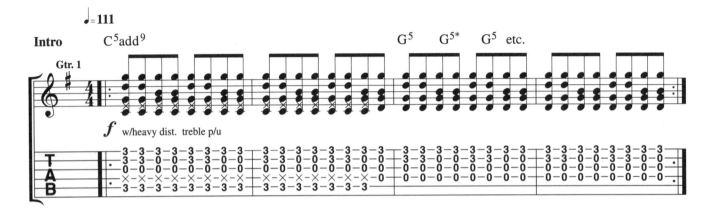

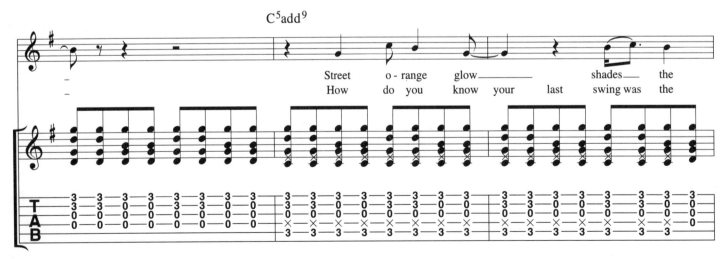

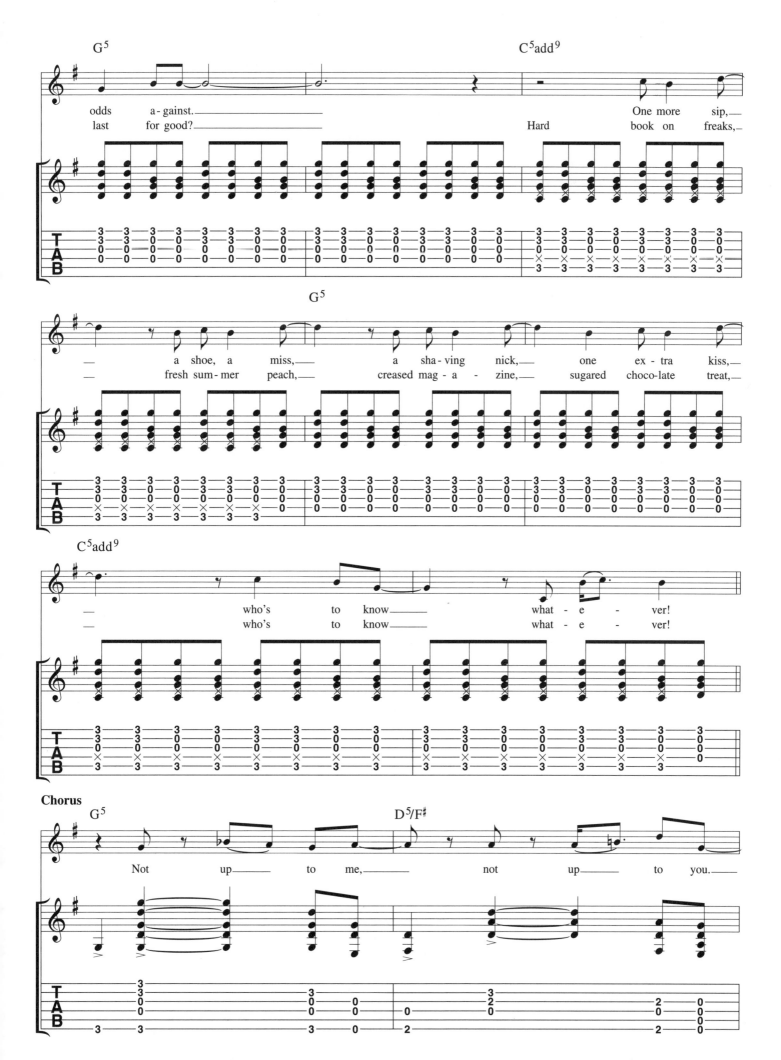

Not up— to me, not up— to you.

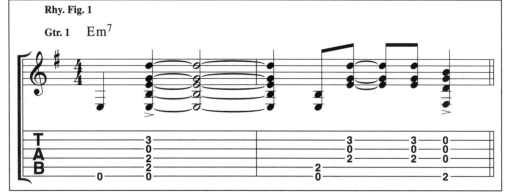

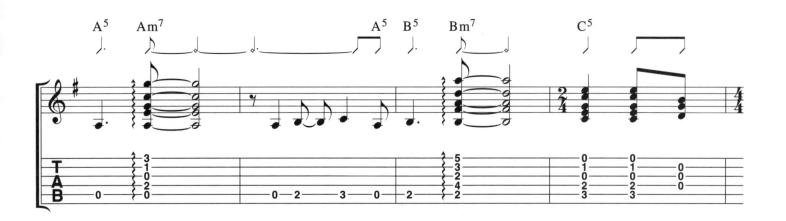

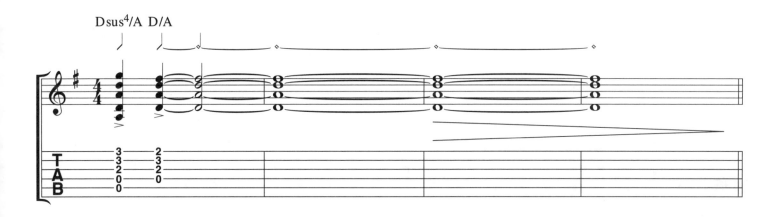

Verse

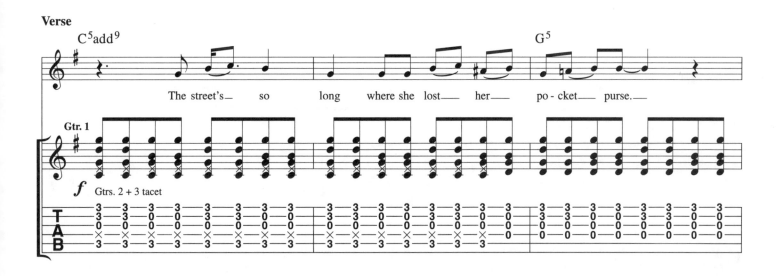

The street's so long where she lost her po-cket purse.

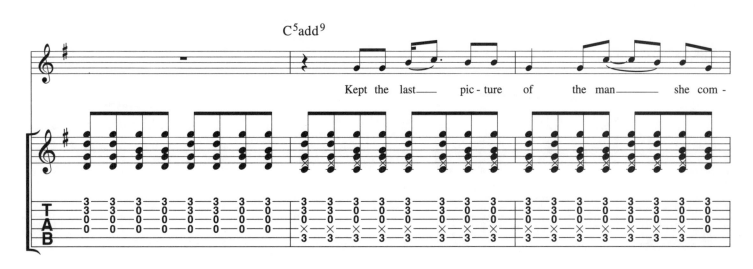

Kept the last pic-ture of the man she com-

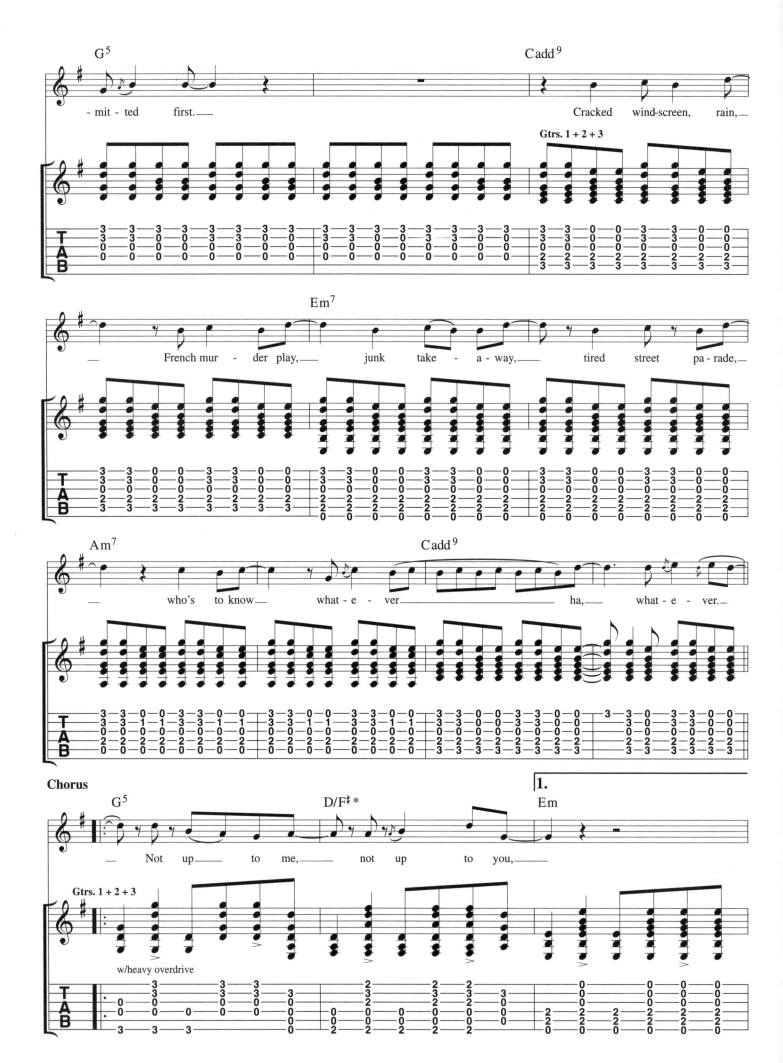

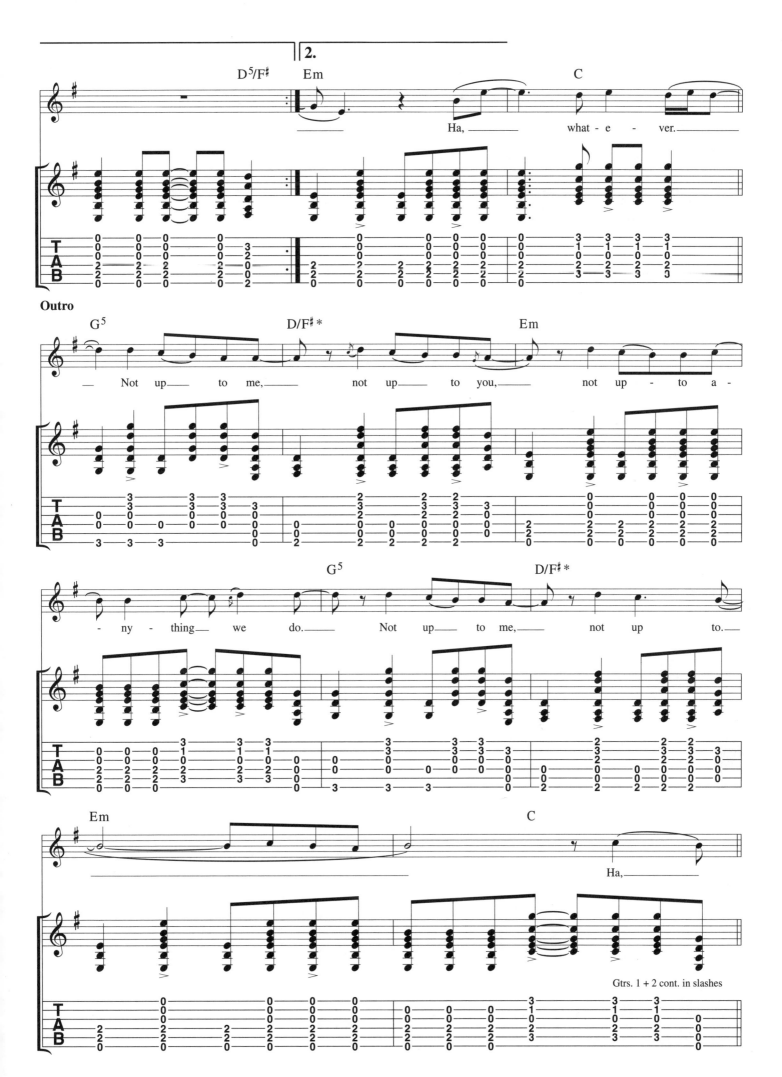

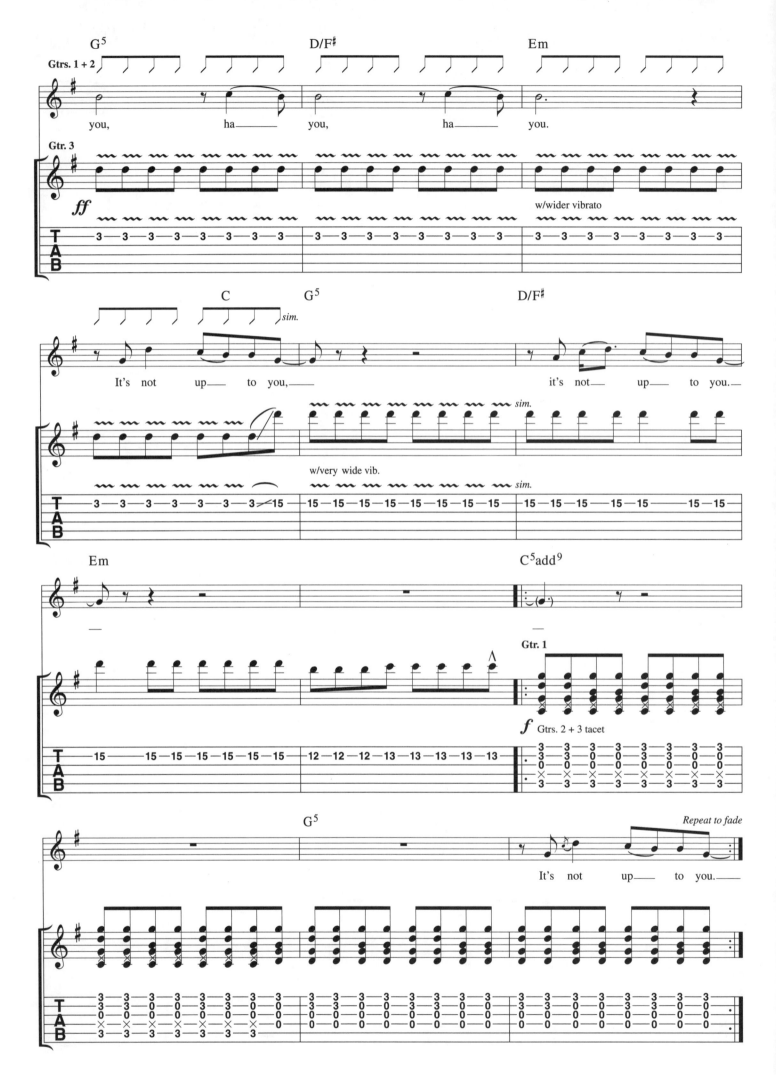

44

same size feet

words by kelly jones. music by kelly jones, richard jones & stuart cable.

49

Verse

Gently
let ring

They found a bo - dy in the lake, may - be— it

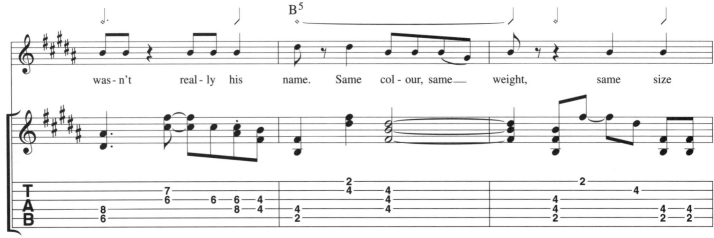

was - n't real - ly his name. Same col - our, same— weight, same size

D.%. al Coda

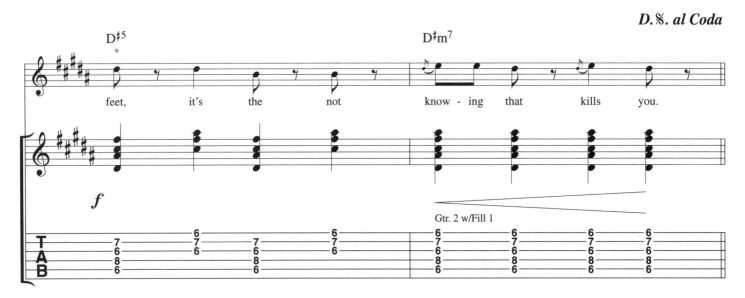

feet, it's the not know - ing that kills you.

Gtr. 2 w/Fill 1

Fill 1

Gtr. 2

f w/dist.

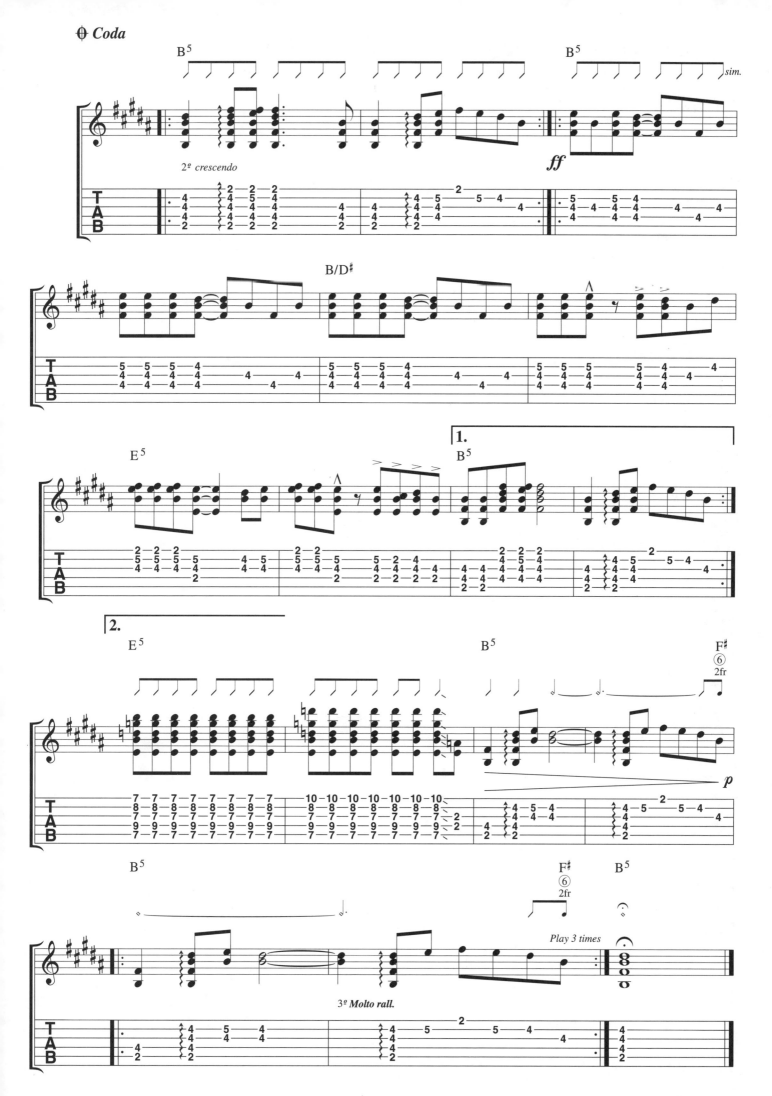

check my eyelids for holes

words by kelly jones. music by kelly jones, richard jones & stuart cable.

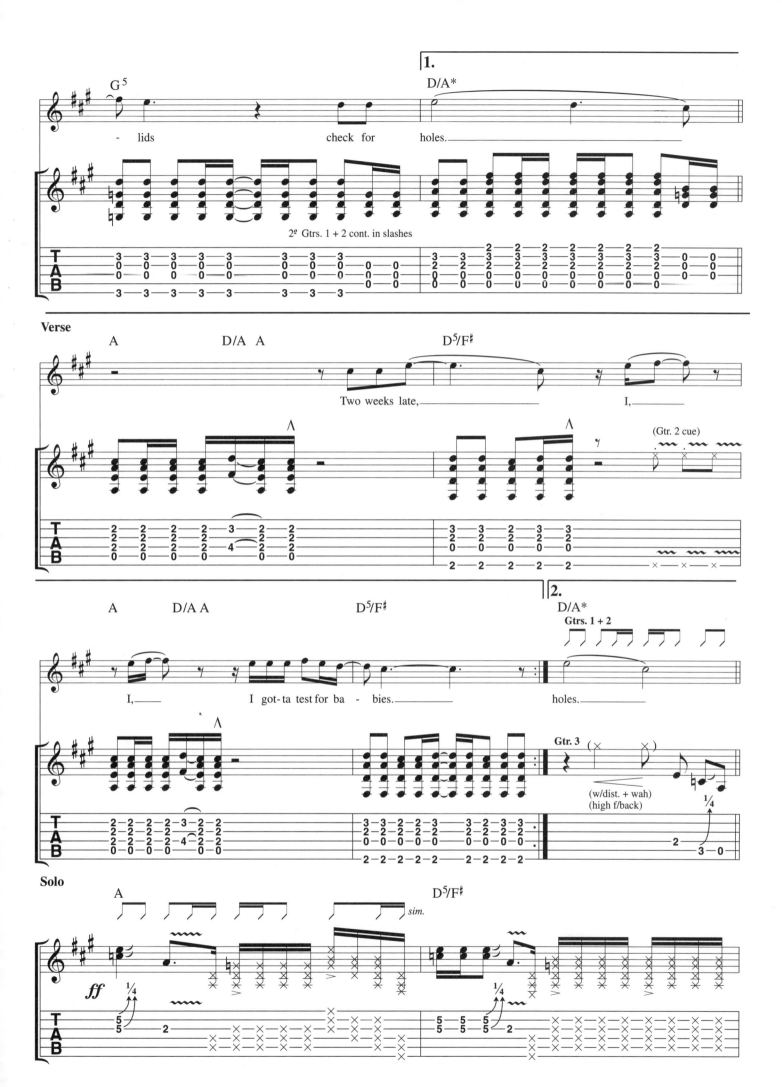

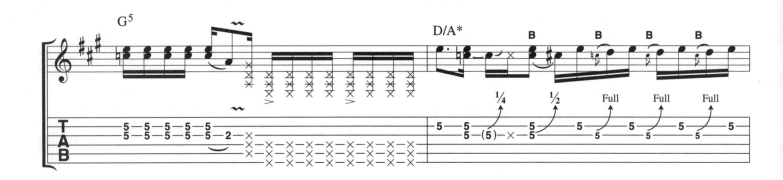

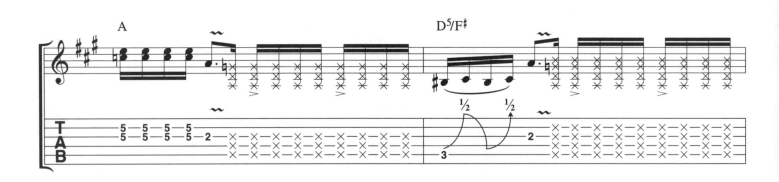

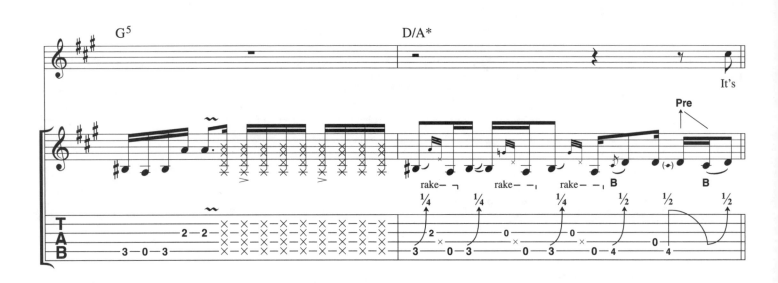

Chorus

time I tried,— tried to check— my, check my eye-

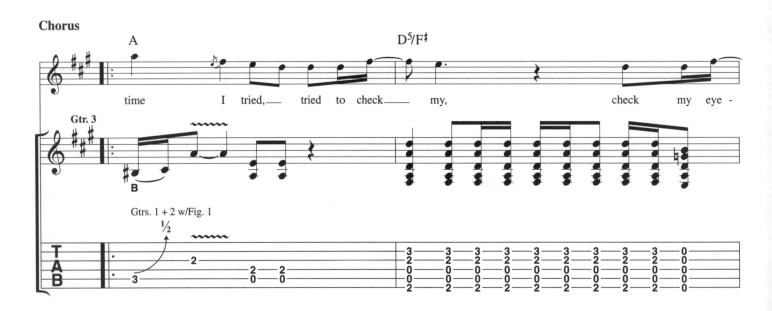

last of the big time drinkers

words by kelly jones. music by kelly jones, richard jones & stuart cable.

beer don't taste the same with - out my name paint - ed on my___

___ glass.___

Instrumental Verse

And I___

Bridge

can't wait for my next drink, the first one is

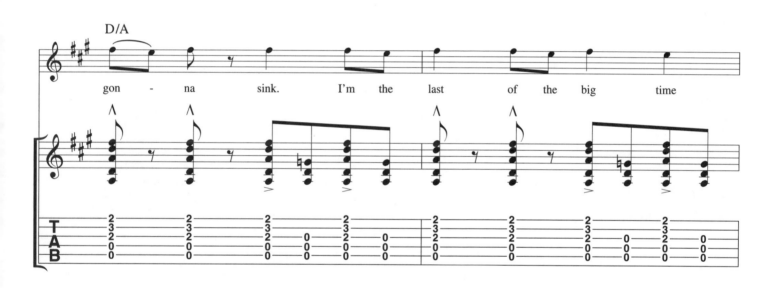

gon - na sink. I'm the last of the big time

Chorus

1. drink - ers, I take pride in my work,
2. - - ers, just gimme hops or the slops, I'm the
3. - - ers, I take pride in my work,

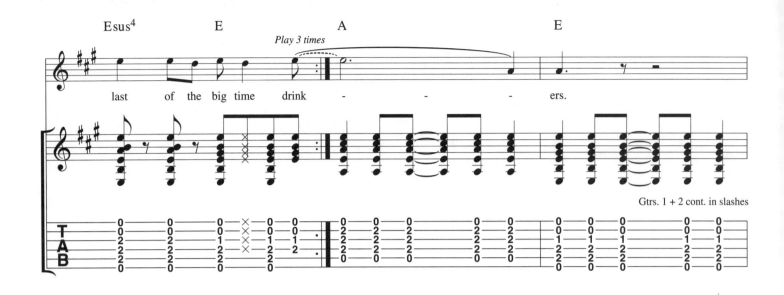

last of the big time drink - - - ers.

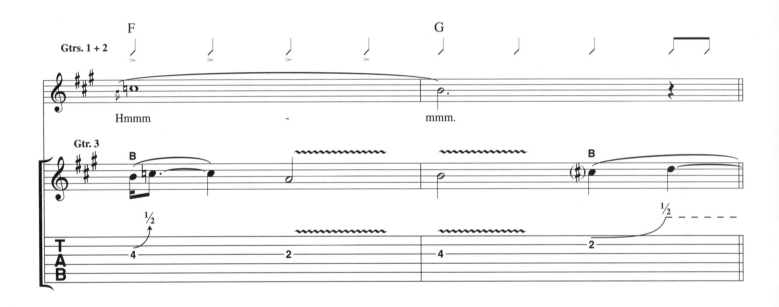

Hmmm - mmm.

Outro

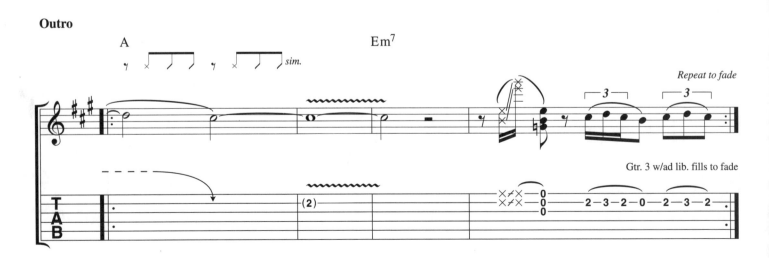

too many sandwiches

words by kelly jones. music by kelly jones, richard jones & stuart cable.

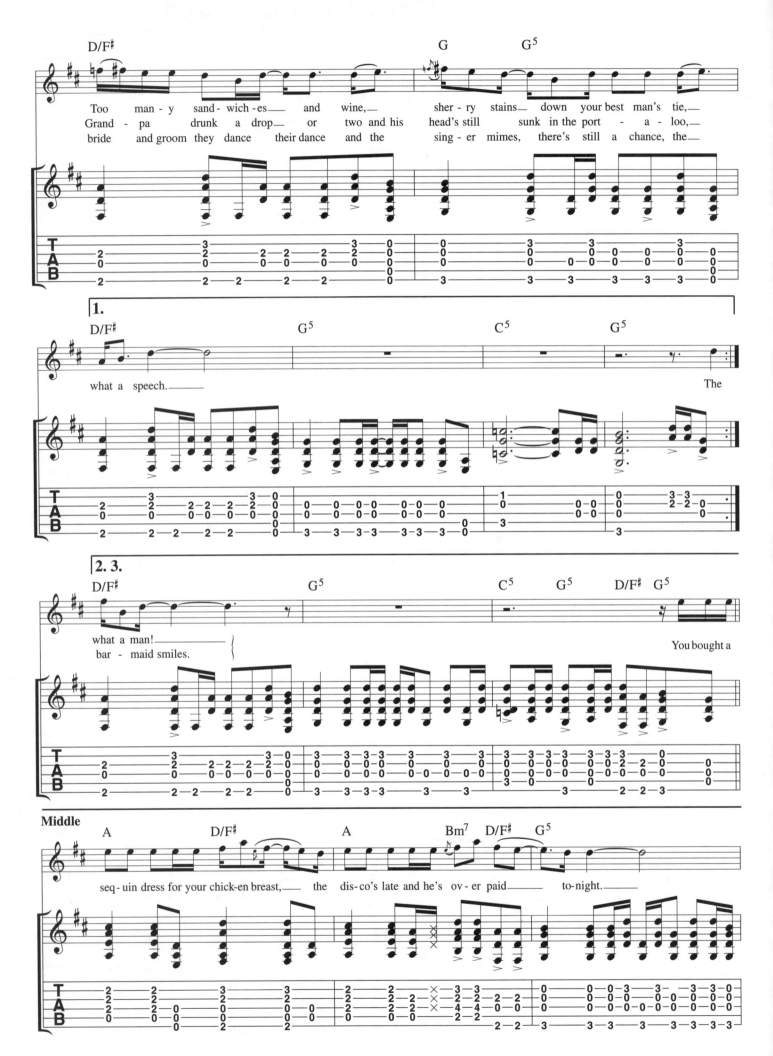

Bridge

Naa na naa,—   naa— na naa.—   (Ohhh)   You bought a

Middle

seq - uin dress for your chick - en breast,— the dis - co's late and he's ov - er paid—

w/clean sound + treble p/u
let ring

— to - night.— Got a

1. diam - ond ring— and a man who sings,— the man who sings made love to the bar -
2. Grand - pa drunk a drop or two,— head's still sunk in the port - a - loo a - gain.
3. bride and groom they danced their dance,— the sing - er mimes there's still a chance

goldfish bowl

words by kelly jones. music by kelly jones, richard jones & stuart cable.

My box - ing ring____ turned to ash.__
A bike_ been used ten times or more.__

...Fig. 1 ends

2ª Gtr. 1 w/Fig. 2 - - - - - - - - - - - - - - - - -

— Red - head
— Grape - vine,

gin - ger bread sells_ tick - ets at the door.__
here's the wife, lays_ down her ro - yal flush.

2ª Gtr. 1 w/Fig. 1 - - - - - - - - - - - - - - - - - -

Fig. 2

Gtr. 1

Middle 8

Chorus

1.

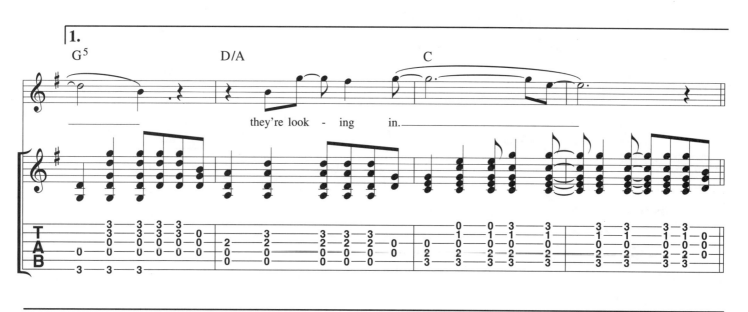

they're look - ing in.

Harmonica Solo

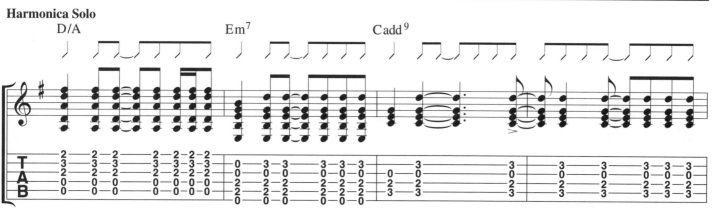

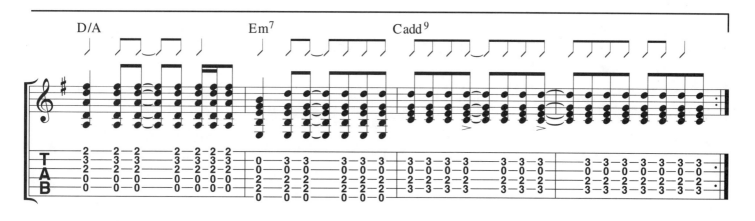

2.

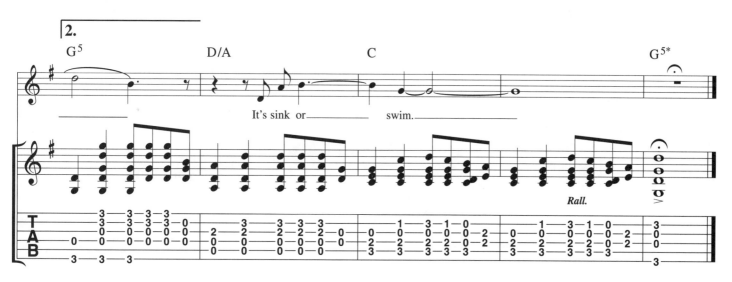

It's sink or_____ swim._____

Rall.

billy daveys daughter

words by kelly jones. music by kelly jones, richard jones & stuart cable.

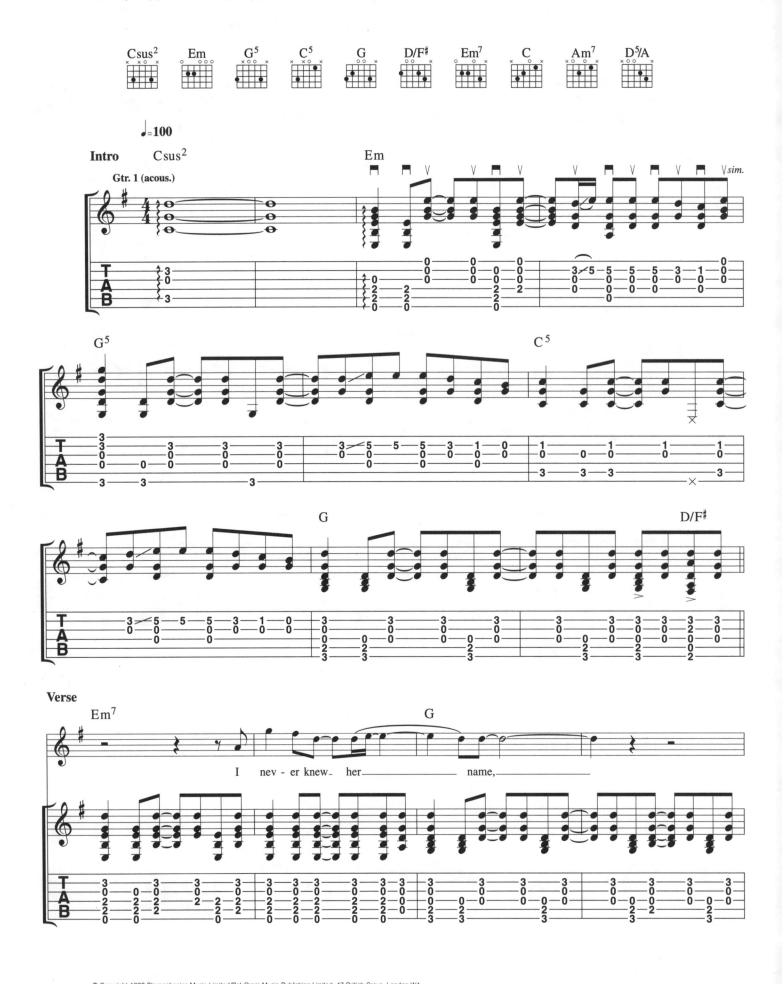

Verse

I nev - er knew her name,

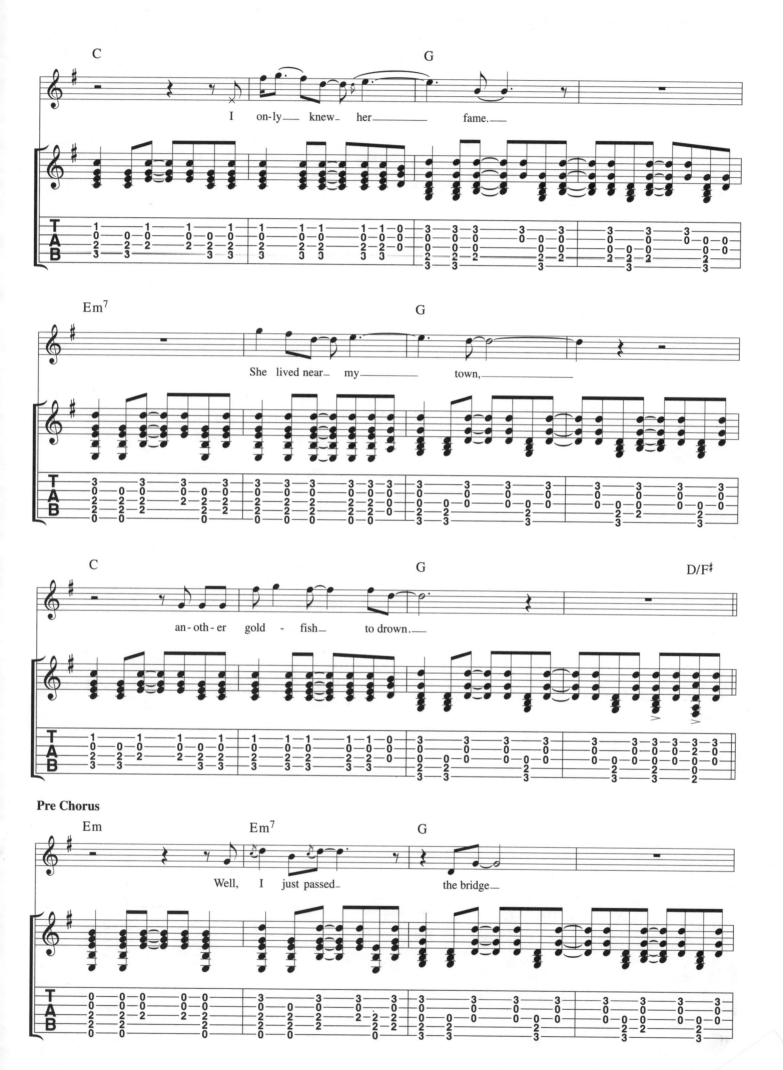

Pre Chorus